Flora of the Fells

Celebrating Cumbria's Mountain Landscapes

Bog   Heath   Flush   Summit

Flora of the Fells Project

Cover photograph: Helvellyn and Striding Edge

Overleaf: Bog-Kentmere, Heath-Carrock Fell, Flush-Helvellyn, Summit-Bowfell

Editing, design and production: Martin Varley

Acknowledgements: Carol Colam, Amanda Conner, Bart Donato, Geoffrey Halliday, Sam and Can Hodgson, Duncan Jeffrey, Alison McAleer, Kath Milnes, Jeremy Roberts, Ian Slater, Ian Taylor, Simon Webb, Jeanne Webb.

Photography: Val Corbett (25 top), Bob Cussen (17 top right, bottom left), English Nature (lichen, 14 top, bottom left), Paul Glendell/English Nature (berries, Flush 7, bottom left, 12, 19 bottom right, 20,), Duncan Jeffrey (17 top left, 17 bottom right), Geoffrey Halliday (26 top right, 35 bottom left, 40 left, 40 middle, 43 right), Rigby Jerram (38 right), Alison McAleer (7 bottom right, 14 bottom right, 15), Barry Stacey (13, 18), Martin Varley (Summit, 7 top right, 8, 23 right, 28, 32 right, 33, 41, 47 top right, 48), Jeanne Webb (7 top left, 11, 19 bottom left, 40 right) Simon Webb (mosses, heather, Heath, 23 left, 24, 25 bottom, 26 left, 26 bottom right, 29, 31, 32 left, 35 top left, 35 top right, 35 bottom right, 38 left, 43 left, 44, 45 left, 47 bottom left, 47 bottom right), Dave Willis/www.mountainsportphoto.com (front cover, Bog, contents page, 21, 36, 39, 45 right, 47 top left)

Illustrations: Map and flowers by Alauna Designs 01539 729023. Map reproduced under copyright licence number AL100033062

ISBN 0-9540506-1-4

If you would like further information about the Flora of the Fells Project please contact:
Martin Varley, Flora of the Fells Project Officer, c/o Friends of the Lake District, Murley Moss, Oxenholme Road, Kendal, Cumbria, LA9 7SS
Tel: 01539 720788
Fax: 01539 730355
E-mail: martin-varley@fld.org.uk
Website: www.floraofthefells.com

Upper Eskdale

Contents

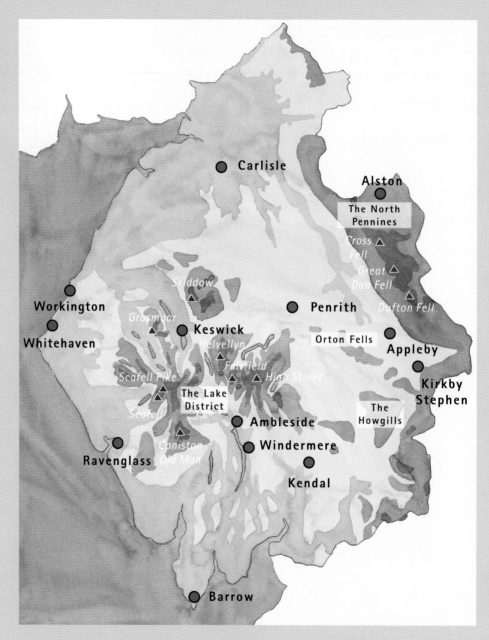

CUMBRIA'S MOUNTAIN LANDSCAPES

mosses   *berries*   *lichen*   *heather*

Foreword

Wandering over the fells, through bracken and rushes and over bent and mat-grass one might well wonder just what is special about Cumbria's mountain flora. But away from the ordinary there are still remnants of the tundra landscape which covered Britain after the last ice age. These are plants which eventually found a refuge in the mountains, on the screes and rock ledges and in the gullies, particularly those facing north and east. Here the right sort of soil could be found, sometimes lime-enriched, with an absence of competition and a cool summer climate, which these sorts of plants need.

These conditions are well met in the eastern coves of the Helvellyn range, easily the best area in the Lake District for alpines. Parsley fern and alpine lady's mantle are conspicuous on the screes while mountain sorrel, lesser meadow rue, yellow, starry and mossy saxifrages, roseroot and hawkweeds feature in the gullies. The early-flowering purple saxifrage grows over the better, more lime-rich rocks, sometimes with the rarer moss campion and alpine mouse-ear chickweed, while if you are very lucky you may chance upon a dwarf willow,

mountain avens or, in the western Lake District, alpine catchfly and oblong woodsia. In the gullies these alpines mingle with more familiar lowland herbs such as red campion, water avens, burnet-saxifrage and even honeysuckle.

The limestone scree and base-rich flushes of the North Pennines add substantially to the flora of the fells. Especially noteworthy are the lovely alpine foxtail grass, marsh saxifrage, alpine forget-me-not and spring gentian, all restricted in England to this area.

It is not just the soil conditions and cool climate that now restrict the rarest upland flora to these habitats. It is also the cumulative effect of centuries of continuous, and latterly, ever-increasing grazing by sheep. In addition, the small and scattered populations are constantly subject to the threats posed by rockfalls and storms and the difficulties which so many seem to have in reproducing by seed. The fact that Cumbria's mountain landscapes still maintain such a diversity of species against the background of these challenges to survival is worthy of celebration.

Geoffrey Halliday
Author of 'A Flora of Cumbria'

Bog   Summit   Flush   Heath

Flora of the Fells

The landscapes and habitats of the Cumbrian fells have not always looked as they do today. The countryside of the Lake District and the North Pennines, which we see on a walk or drive through, is only a moment in time. The sheltered woods and steep gills, the wet bogs and windswept summits look as if they have always been there; they seem peaceful places. But beneath this tranquillity lurks an ecological battleground, where the flora of the fells has to fight for survival.

If we compress recent ecological history into a 24-hour period then this will give us some impression of the scale of this continual change going on throughout Cumbria's mountain landscapes. Our day begins around

12,000 years ago. Britain is just emerging from the last ice age, a time when glaciers carved out Cumbria's valleys and sculpted its peaks, laying the foundations of the landscape of today.

The retreat of the ice sheets opened up huge areas for colonisation by plants . At this time, there was no English Channel and what we now call arctic-alpine flora would have covered much of the continent. Arctic-alpine flowers are poor at competing, but can survive in harsh environments and are now more commonly associated with the Arctic and alpine mountain ranges. Under the tundra-like conditions prevailing at the end of the last ice age, arctic-alpine flora took advantage

Alpine bartsia was first discovered in England in 1688 at a site in Cumbria near Orton by John Ray, one

Four ages of change to Cumbria's mountain landscapes compressed into a single day. Top left: 1 am – the end of the ice age. Top right: 10 am – the advance of the forests. Bottom left: 5.30 pm – the coming of the bogs. Bottom right: 11 pm – the arrival of man

of the founding fathers of British botany *Alpine lady's mantle was believed to possess magical*

Borrowdale

of the cool climate and limited competition for
space, expanding their distribution in the wake of the
vanishing glaciers. Woody plants such as dwarf willow,
juniper and dwarf birch thrived and so did flowers like
roseroot, mountain sorrel and purple saxifrage. This was
the golden era for arctic-alpine plants in Cumbria.

As the climate gradually warmed so the reign of the
cold-loving species rapidly waned. The story of post-
glacial vegetation change was one of wholesale retreat
and extinction as wave upon wave of new species
dominated the landscape. The primary invaders were
heath species, such as bilberry and crowberry, closely
followed by successive reigns of woodland kings
beginning with the birch. Dominant species came and
went until ultimately, a broadleaved forest, mainly of
hazel, elm and oak, took control of the land.

Pollen records from lake sediments and bogs in Cumbria
suggest that by mid-morning on our ecological day
broadleaved woodland had spread across Cumbria,
up to at least 600 m. This arboreal advance forced an
exodus of arctic-alpine flora onto the mountain tops.
Here the remnants sought refuge in habitats on ledges
and scree and around tarns and gills, where the climate
was cooler and there was less competition for space.

qualities after sixteenth-century scientists discovered that dew collected in the folds of its partly closed

Alpine lady's mantle

(otherwise known as *Alchemilla alpina*)

What does it look like? Alpine lady's mantle is a low creeping plant. Its leaves spread like fingers and have silvery undersides. Its unassuming pale yellow-green flowers grow in clusters on long stems.

Where does it grow? It favours steep, dry slopes below crags and also grows on and below stone walls, on rock ledges and on the open fellside. It is not found in Cumbria in the North Pennines.

When can you see it? It flowers between June and August.

What's so special about it? It is one of the most conspicious plants of the Lake District fells. It takes its name from the medicinal use of its dried leaves to relieve the discomfort of menopause and excessive menstruation.

leaves ❋ *'Thine eyes are like the bilberry, full and fresh upon the brae. Thy cheeks shall blush*

Juniper

(otherwise known as *Juniperus communis*)

What does it look like? Juniper grows in a variety of forms, as bushes or small trees up to 3m tall. Its branches have spiky green needles and the berries start off green, then turn blue-black when ripe.

Where does it grow? It likes rocky, stony places and moors, particularly on valley sides in the Lake District, but hardly occurs in Cumbria in the North Pennines.

When can you see it? It flowers in May and June, but can be seen all year round.

What's so special about it? Juniper's main claim to fame is as a flavouring in gin. It also gives a gamey taste to whisky. In fact it is something of a wonder plant, being an ingredient in nearly 300 pharmaceutical products, mostly as a diuretic and for stomach and digestive disorders.

Mountain avens

Slowly, the forests at higher altitudes underwent a new transformation to grassland and heather moorland. This process of change was accelerated by a climatic shift towards wetter, cooler conditions around teatime on our ecological day, which led to the development of extensive upland bog, particularly on the gently contoured North Pennines.

The final chapter in the story of Cumbria's landscape is much more recent. The impact of Neolithic farming began a process of change in the uplands which continued, albeit slowly, with the advent of the Celtic and Roman cultures. The Norse settlers finally opened up the valleys as they sought more and more land for grazing. By the time of the Norman Conquest, there was probably very little natural forest remaining.

Only from this time, about an hour before midnight on our ecological day, does the landscape start to look familiar to us. In this last hour, and in particular during the last few moments, high numbers of sheep and other grazing animals on the fells have brought about a change almost as dramatic as the forest clearances.

Colour, variety and diversity have slowly disappeared

Human activity enters our ecological day after lunch, when the first Neolithic farmers arrived in Cumbria around 3000 BC. The forests, which had dominated the Cumbrian mountain landscape for 4500 years, were gradually felled and burned, leaving traces of charcoal which have been recovered from studies of peat sediments. Over the next thousand years the impact of these clearances compounded natural ongoing processes like soil erosion and leaching of nutrients.

in Lancashire used bog asphodel to dye their hair yellow, giving rise to the local name of maiden

The botanist

For thirty years I tramped the high moors of the Cross Fell range. I often used to wonder how the mountain vegetation might respond to a reduction in the severe sheep grazing to which the tops had been routinely subjected for so long. When the fell sheep were lost through foot-and-mouth culling, that chance arose.

By the late summer of 2002, vegetation had had two seasons of untrammelled growth. An astonishing sight was revealed! Over huge areas, the previous monotonous stretches of mat-grass and rushes were now enlivened by many other species reasserting themselves, no longer nibbled down to the ground by the selective appetites of the sheep. In the endless breeze, cotton-sedges made billowing white swathes, tall grass heads swayed gracefully and innumerable mountain flowers starred the turf with white, pink and yellow. Some of the rarest and most significant species, such as marsh saxifrage and alpine foxtail, flowered in unprecedented profusion. The latter appeared in areas where hitherto it had been overlooked.

The high rills were made pink by sheets of hairy stonecrop and chickweed willowherb, both usually inconspicuous plants. A local botanist found two colonies of a sedge, known on Scottish mountains, but never before seen in England. It is clear that these plants contrived to outlast the epoch of over-grazing, most usually by having creeping stems at or below ground level that even the close-nibbling sheep failed to reach. Now, I believe, it is time to cherish what we have left, and perhaps allow these special mountain species to re-take some of the ground they have lost.

Jeremy Roberts, Wetheral

hair ❀ *If a woman went down on one knee, plucked nine roots of butterwort and knotted them into*

from the upland scene as a new ecological challenge has unfolded in which there is a growing risk that the activities of man may overwhelm natural processes. The flora of the fells is more than just something to add interest to a walk, it is an indicator of the health of Cumbria's mountain landscapes.

This ongoing saga of dominance and decline, of the rise and fall of ecological empires, is the background to the flora of the fells. It has produced our wide variety of landscapes and habitats, each distinctive, some unique, but all special to the Cumbrian uplands.

Wild woods

Although Cumbria's mountains were once heavily wooded there are only a handful of places where it is

Sheep gathering in the fells above Kirkby Stephen

a ring, it was said that she could put this hoop in her mouth and the man she kisses would be servile to

Cumbria's ancient woodlands are home to some of our rarest mosses, lichens and liverworts

still possible to get a glimpse of what this landscape must once have been like. These places are relics of ancient woodland which avoided the clearances of the Middle Ages. They are areas of high rainfall where the barks of oak, ash and hazel drip with moss. Draped like a cloak over steep valley sides, their understorey is broken with lichen-crusted blocks and rocky outcrops. Moisture-loving ferns cling to the sides of gills which divide the woodlands, tumbling down waterfalls and ravines.

This feeling of the wild wood, of how the slopes of the Cumbrian fells must have looked in the millennia before man, is best experienced in Borrowdale where a red squirrel can go from Keswick to Seathwaite almost without touching the ground. In the woods of Lodore, Seathwaite and Seatoller you will find luxuriant habitats for lichens, mosses and liverworts, with many species rare in Britain and others not found anywhere else in England.

Specialised ferns, like the oak and beech ferns, hide in the shady corners. There are other good examples of ancient woodlands at Glencoyne Wood by Ullswater, Side Wood in Ennerdale, in the Duddon and Rusland valleys and around Coniston.

her forever   ✸   *In one parish in the Berwyn mountains of Wales cloudberries were so hard to come by*

The guesthouse owner

One of the joys of running a guesthouse is the opportunity that it provides to share my love of the fells with like-minded visitors. The wonderful thing about living here, rather than just visiting once or twice a year, is that you see the same landscapes in all weathers and all seasons. With a seven day-a-week job for most of the year I probably have fewer long days out on the fells than I did as a holiday maker. On the other hand I get out on the fells around Keswick for an hour or two most days.

In the spring particularly, I love to go through Great Wood in Borrowdale, watching the change as green shoots appear among the leaf litter and one small white flower is replaced by another, until the carpets of bluebells and wild garlic take over. In the early summer leaving Great Wood for the path across the fell below Falcon Crags, where sheep have been excluded for the last three years, majestic spikes of foxglove stand tall in a sea of green bracken while a variety of wild flowers have colonised the grassy clearings.

By July the top of Walla Crag is purple with heather, sweetly aromatic on a summer afternoon. Once autumn arrives with the gold, brown and red hues of the trees and bracken glowing in the soft sunlight I know that the peace and quiet of winter can't be far away.

The mountain landscapes provide a wonderful, ever-changing mosaic of light and shade on hills and across lakes. Every day is different; every season has its own delights.

Carol Colam, Cumbria House, Keswick

that anyone collecting a quart of berries and giving them to the parson on the parish saint's day was let

Bilberry

Collecting bilberries was once a way of life, with picking being celebrated by the whole familiy in early August. On the Isle of Man the event became an excuse for riotous games and lovemaking and there are many accounts of clergy preaching against the practice.

Its influence on our culture is reflected in the variety of local names given to the plant which include bleaberry, blueberry, hurtleberry and wimberry.

In Cumbria it has even left its mark on the landscape with a Bleaberry Knott in Langdale, a Bleaberry Fell near Keswick as well as a

Cloudberry

The first record of the plant was by Thomas Penny, a sixteenth-century botanist who took too much notice of local folklore. The plants, he said, were called knotberries or cloudberries. Knotberries, because the fruit looked like knots; cloudberries because the plants grew on mountains permanently covered in clouds.

He was wrong on both counts as each name is simply a derivation meaning 'hill berry'.

Plants can be found amongst the bogs of the North Pennines, and where they fruit, this can be used to make a pleasant jam,

Cranberry

Cranberries are used as a favourite filling for pies, and are excellent as jams and in cranberry sauce. Their love of boggy places has given them a variety of names, including marsh wort, fen-berry and moss-berry.

The plants are well adapted to their habitat. Bog water has few nutrients, but the plants' waxy leaves transpire quickly allowing large volumes of water to pass through and compensate for the low levels of nutrients.

Their delicate red flowers are borne on slender stalks resembling a crane's head and neck, which is perhaps

Crowberry

It is possible to eat the small, black berries which grow on the plant, but they have an unpleasant acidic taste. The fleshy, juicy fruits are best left to grouse and other moorland birds who feed on them when they ripen in late summer.

The crowberry is a common sight on Cumbria's mountains on crags and in moorland. It often occurs alongside heather and bilberry.

The plant's long slender branches hug the ground and spread rapidly, choking other plants out as they do.

Bilberry

Cloudberry

Cranberry

Crowberry

berries

lichen

mosses

heather

Hell Gill Force, Mallerstang

Sparkling water

Many of our most striking flowers need a good supply of nutrients, in particular lime, which comes from the soil that in turn is derived from the underlying rock. In the bright, new world that unfolded at the end of the last ice age there was a fresh supply of nutrient-rich soil, which allowed arctic-alpine plants to flourish.

However, after centuries of rain, much of this richness has leached away. In the Lake District new soil formed from the underlying rocks is generally low in nutrients, apart from a few lime-rich pockets in the central and southern fells. In the North Pennines, the extensive bogs are naturally poor in nutrients, but have their own characteristic flora. Compounding this process, across all of Cumbria's mountains, the continued intensive

off paying tithes for a year ❋ *Fir clubmoss was said to be such a strong purgative, it could bring on*

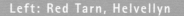

Left: Red Tarn, Helvellyn

Below left: Yellow mountain saxifrage

Below: Knock Ore Gill, Great Dun Fell

giddiness and convulsions, and in some even an abortion ✤ *Stag's horn clubmoss was also known as*

Yellow marsh saxifrage

nutrient-rich rock. Such places occur even in the most unpromising grassland, heath or bog. The bright greens, browns and reds of mosses and liverworts provide splashes of colour as a canvas for an often rich variety of flowers, such as starry saxifrage and yellow mountain saxifrage.

Fine examples can be seen in the North Pennines on the flanks of Cross Fell and on the fellsides around Orton and Asby. To find the best flora here you may need to leave the beaten path and explore the rills and gullies below the summits of the highest fells. Here the geology favours the flora. The dominant blanket bog is resting on a layer of limestone. The limestone helps to provide the conditions necessary for the growth of more specialised flowers as water draining through the bog dissolves the minerals in the bedrock before seeping back out onto the surface.

grazing of sheep and other domestic animals has further degraded the soils by opening them up to the erosive forces of wind and rain.

There are, however, still pockets of brightness, particularly where water comes to the surface in springs and flushes having percolated through

There is often a pink haze of hairy stonecrop around these flushes in early spring, alongside plants like alpine willowherb, mossy saxifrage and pale forget-me-not. There are even a few places where the rare yellow marsh saxifrage can be seen. It is not found anywhere else in Cumbria and most of its sites in Britain are on these mineral-rich flushes of the Pennines.

vegetable sulphur; it was used by theatres as a special effects powder during the nineteenth and twentieth

The fellwalker

I enjoy walking in the fells, but realistically I've spent more time looking up at them than looking down from them. I'm sure that in our busy world I'm not alone in this.

I love to walk from the National Trust car park between Grasmere and Rydal Water follow the path to the footbridge and cross to the other side of the stream. My favoured route then takes the right hand path at the fork along the side of the river. You can at this point see a mix of oak, silver birch and beech trees and if you pay attention you may see a variety of birds from treecreeper to robin, wren to mallard.

However, there is considerable pleasure to be had in just listening to the sounds of the stream bubbling beside you, watching the light play through the trees on the water and feeling the wind and probably the rain on your face. A few moments of serenity, being encompassed by your environment, beautiful but different every time.

Then you are out of the trees, walking along the lake shore and looking north over Grasmere towards the mountains. Grasmere nestles snugly in the bottom of a basket of hills. None of them are particularly remarkable in their own right, but together they form an ever-changing symphony of colour and form throughout the year. They even look good in the rain – and not many of us can say that!

Amanda Connor, Kendal

centuries ✳ *Cotton-grass was collected by children in Scotland to supply wound dressings during the*

Sea pink

(otherwise known as thrift or *Armeria maritima*)

What does it look like? Sea pink has narrow, tufty leaves out of which grow clusters of pink flowers, held aloft on long stalks.

Where does it grow? It is usually found on coastal cliffs and headlands, but on Cumbria's fells it makes an unexpected appearance on the ledges of Pillar, Steeple, Scafell Pike and Helvellyn and on old lead workings around Alston.

When can you see it? It flowers between April and October.

What's so special about it? Sea pink is one of the few plants which occurs only on the coast and in the mountains. This is because it can tolerate the harsh conditions in both habitats. Until James Backhouse confirmed that it was sea pink growing on Scafell in the nineteenth century, the plant was thought to be a different species, known locally as Scafell pink.

First World War ❋ *Woven stems of fairy flax placed under milk storage jugs were believed to prevent*

Plants of the pasture

If you go for a walk in the fells the chances are you will
spend much of your time crossing wide areas of closely
cropped grassland. This landscape is a far cry from
when woodland penetrated high up the mountain sides,
often covering the summits. Heathland was one of the
earliest colonists following the Neolithic clearances, but
a combination of heavy grazing and burning ultimately
led to grassland becoming widespread.

The acid nature of the underlying rock throughout
much of the Lake District and the continued intensive

Spring sandwort

Species-rich limestone grassland at Whitbarrow

the milk from being spirited away by fairies ❋ *Goldenrod chopped up and mixed with butter was used*

The conservationist

The first few years of the new millennium have seen a dramatic reduction in the numbers of sheep grazing the North Pennines. After years of heavy grazing the balance has now shifted in favour of rich mixtures of heathers, mosses, lichens and colourful grasslands. The monotonous turf of grazing-resistant species, such as mat-grass and heath rush, has had its day.

At the northern tip of the Pennines, land around the headwaters of the River Gelt is being grazed with far fewer sheep. Woodland regeneration is being promoted on the deeper soils of the valley sides. Wood pastures are being re-created where cattle will gently graze amongst spreading trees.

The open blanket bogs around the Moorhouse National Nature Reserve will be grazed by half the number of sheep following a buy-out of grazing rights and entry into agreements which support farming at a less intensive level. Change is also afoot on the highest ground around Cross Fell. Here the commoners have worked together to reduce flock sizes and they are now managing land under the Countryside Stewardship Scheme.

On the fells above Brough a change of use of the common land, associated with the demands of military training, will focus grazing on the limestone grasslands and away from the more vulnerable blanket bogs.

The North Pennines from Brough to Brampton and Stainmore to the Tyne, is now being managed to benefit the flora and breeding birds. Three years ago we could not have believed that such change could ever happen. The pieces of a landscape-scale jigsaw puzzle are falling into place; the outlook is for a healthy and blooming Pennines.

Simon Webb, English Nature, Kendal

in the treatment of fresh wounds *A bed of heather was believed to have the power to give restful*

Pastures and open woodland at Smardale

grazing by animals has limited the flora of these pastures.

Wild thyme

However, where conditions are right, the flora is ready to respond. There are pockets in the Lakeland fells where the geology has increased the mineral content of the soil, such as on the fells above Haweswater and Derwent Water. Here amongst a diverse mixture of grasses, flowers and mosses are found more unusual species like alpine lady's mantle.

In the south and east of the county, particularly on the North Pennine fells above Dufton and Warcop, and also around Kirkby Stephen, the geology changes from that of the central Lake District. Here, in summer, you can walk amongst pastures fragrant with the scent of wild thyme and across some fine examples of mountain-top limestone grassland and limestone pavement. On the

sleep and the practice of sleeping with a sprig of heather under the pillow still continues ❁ *There*

Top left: Spring gentian

Top right: Alpine forget-me-not

Bottom right: Mountain pansy

slopes above Helbeck, near Brough, where there is less grazing and the ground is rockier, a carpet of rockrose and biting stonecrop can colour the ground yellow in early summer.

The higher slopes provide a refuge for some of Cumbria's arctic-alpine plants, clinging on to survival since the last ice age. Here you will see mossy saxifrage

is evidence that heather ale has been brewed in Scotland for over two thousand years. It can be made by

Bird's-Eye Primrose

(otherwise known as *Primula farinosa*)

What does it look like? Bird's-eye primrose resembles its more familiar cousin only in the shape of its flowers. But they are more delicate and pink in colour, clustered together on a single stalk growing up to 15 cm long.

Where does it grow? Britain's population is centred on the North Pennines, which is Cumbria's stronghold. It likes damp meadows and boggy ground, mostly on limestone.

When can you see it? It is best enjoyed between May and June.

What's so special about it? It is one of Cumbria's most distinctive mountain plants. The middle of each flower has a yellow spot, giving it the look of a bird's eye, from which it takes its name.

mixing an infusion of heather flowers with ginger, hops, golden syrup and yeast Juniper berries are

Limestone pavement on Grange Scar, near Orton

used to flavour gin, but its oil was also used to bring on an abortion. Hence gin became known as 'mother's

Heavy metal tolerant plants colonising a spoil heap near Alston

Summit   Bog   Flush   Heath

and mountain pansy, and perhaps the deep blue splash of spring gentian. In a handful of places are clusters of rare alpine forget-me-not, a plant found only at one other site in Britain.

As well as being a stronghold for the bird's-eye primrose, the landscape around Orton has spectacular expanses of limestone pavement. Peer down into the cracks and crevices and you will see that they are teeming with moisture-loving ferns.

On the moors around Alston, where intensive lead mining has released copper, zinc and chromium into the soil, a different type of upland pasture has developed. Here, more unusual plants, like spring sandwort and alpine pennycress, tolerant of high levels of toxic heavy metals, further diversify the flora of the fells.

ruin' ❈ Dried berries of juniper are said to yield a yellow dye ❈ There is a long held belief

Bell Heather

(otherwise known as *Erica cinerea*)

What does it look like? Most of us use the name heather to describe the purple-pink plant that covers the fellsides in late summer. But this colourful display is often a mixture of three plants: bell heather, ling and cross-leaved heath.

Where does it grow? It grows throughout Cumbria, but is a choosy heathland species, preferring drier places on rock outcrops or along gillsides.

When can you see it? Its colour spectacular runs from July to September.

What's so special about it? Walkers would do well to seek out bell heather when crossing boggy land as the plant grows on the driest tussocks. Boiled in water and applied warm to the crown of the head or temples it is said to be a remedy for sleeplessness.

that lousewort was so-called because it infested sheep with lice The leaves of mountain avens

A splash of colour

Think of a colour to describe late summer in the hills of Cumbria and many of us would imagine heather moorland and a swathe of purple on the fellside. Yet if you look more closely at the best upland heaths you will see they are made up not only of heather, but also other dwarf shrubs, sometimes with stunted growth due to the climate. In many places the heath forms a carpet of intertwined branches rich in lichens and mosses. Here the purples and pinks form a mosaic with greens, yellows and greys extending high up the mountain slopes from the upper limits of the valley-side woodlands .

There are good sites on the Skiddaw fells, the fells around Watendlath and amongst the mountains north of Buttermere. Bell heather, ling and cross-leaved heath dominate but, depending upon the types of soils, you can also find bilberry, crowberry, cowberry and, more rarely, bearberry. The bilberry heaths of the Buttermere fells are more extensive than at any other site in north-west England.

But there is a delicate equlibrium between heather moorland and upland grassland. Overgrazing by sheep

Heathland with juniper, Carrock Fell

look like oak leaves, hence its latin name Dryas, after the dryad, the wood nymph of the oak 🌿 *The*

can easily upset this balance leaving deserts of mat-grass, with heathland species being forced to retreat to inaccessible ledges or being lost completely. There

The impact of overgrazing at Little Asby Common

The best upland heathlands are a multicoloured mosaic of diverse plants

are striking examples in the landscape of the contrast between overgrazed grassland and healthy heathland separated by a wall or fence. The fresh shoots of many shrubs are often nibbled by grazing animals before they have opportunity to fruit.

Bog glorious bog!

For most of us bog is a far from popular landscape. At first glance its monotony fails to inspire the eye, its dampness is unappealing underfoot. Yet Britain holds

pansy at my feet/ Doth the same tale repeat/ Whither is fled the visionary gleam?/ Where is it now the

The farmer

Much of the Lake District is an Environmental Sensitive Area. This is a scheme through which farmers are paid to farm in an environmentally-sensitive way. In the rest of Cumbria environmentally-sensitive farming is encouraged through another scheme called the Countryside Stewardship Scheme.

Farmers in the Environmentally Sensitive Area can enter into the scheme at different levels of commitment. The majority of farmers in the Lake District have entered the scheme, but mostly at its basic level. It has been operating since 1993 and has already been shown to benefit both farmers and the countryside.

Sam and Can Hodgson farm at Glencoyne Farm and have opted to make more than just a basic commitment. 'We believe that good quality farming doesn't need to be at the expense of the environment', says Sam. They have been at Glencoyne Farm for seven years and have already seen a change in the landscape. After having agreed to reduce the number of sheep, they keep they have seen heather returning to hillsides previously grazed bare and this is encouraging more and more wildlife. The sheep are benefitting too. They are healthier and more productive, cost less to look after, and achieve a good price at the market.

'For many years farmers have been encouraged to increase production', says Sam, 'but farming is changing and people are starting to realise that it can't continue like it is. We are trying to show that there is an alternative which maintains traditional farming and enhances the landscape.'

CUMBRIA'S RARE FLORA

Alpine Bartsia

Although alpine bartsia is common throughout the mountains of Scandinavia and central Europe, it now occurs at only a handful of sites in Britain. Cumbria has a couple of sites on the limestone around Orton.

The great plant-namer, Carl Linnaeus, christened the plant after the German botanist Johannes Bartsch, who died from tropical fever after taking up a post in Surinam. Linnaeus had recommended Bartsch for the post, after he himself had turned it down for fear that he would not survive in the climate. Naming a plant after him perhaps helped appease Linnaeus' guilt.

Alpine Catchfly

Fossils of alpine catchfly from the last ice age have been found as far south as Essex and the Isle of Man, but a major decline in its distribution has left only two sites remaining in Britain. One is in Scotland and the other in Cumbria, near Keswick.

Alpine catchfly is able to thrive in soils with heavy metals that are too toxic for other plants. In Sweden it occurs on spoil heaps of disused copper, lead and zinc mines. This unusual tolerance led Scandinavian botanists to christen the plant 'kisplant', pyrite plant, or 'kobberblomst', copper flower.

Moss Campion

South of the Scottish Highlands moss campion only occurs in the Lake District and Snowdonia. It favours ledges and steep slabs with the few remaining plants found on the crags of Helvellyn, High Street and Scafell.

The flowers vary in colour from white through to deep rose. In the Arctic, where extensive areas of moss campion develop, flowers on the south side of cushions have been observed to open first. By the time the flowers on the north side open the south side flowers are producing fruit. Thus the plant provides a very crude compass to anyone lost in the Arctic wastes.

Purple Saxifrage

Cushions of purple saxifrage have survived on only a few sheltered ledges and gullies on the high fells of the Lake District, where it seeks out nutrient-rich pockets in the otherwise nutrient-poor rock.

It flowers early in the year and so is easy to overlook, even by those who seek it out. In the Alps it has even been known to flower beneath the snow.

Purple saxifrage is one of the hardiest arctic-alpine plants, with a claim for being the most northerly occurring. It has been recorded at 83°N on the north-east coast of Greenland.

Alpine bartsia

Alpine catchfly

Moss campion

Purple saxifrage

Treading carefully on Stony Cove Pike

ten per cent of the world's bogs and in many parts of the Cumbrian fells they are difficult to get away from. Taking advantage of climate change towards wetter and cooler conditions, bogs began their irresistible advance into the uplands during the Bronze Age. In places, birch and alder woodlands were able to resist for a time, but the bogs' slow expansion eventually overwhelmed them. Their fight is recorded in ancient trunks and fragments of trees which have been recovered from the lower layers of peat bogs.

Often termed 'blanket bog', reflecting the nature of its dominance in the landscape, this habitat occurs throughout Cumbria's uplands. To really test the waterproofing of your boots head for the North Pennines and the moors around Cross Fell or north towards Stainmore, where the gently sloping topography has allowed extensive areas of bog to form.

Often during the summer, familiar white tufts of cotton-grass ripple over the surface. Look more closely and you will find other mountain plants which have made their home in this sodden landscape. Cross-leaved heath, cowberry, crowberry, bog asphodel and the tiny red-trimmed leaves of the insect-eating sundew can all

Caledonian railway in 1848 coincided with the near extinction of the oblong woodsia in the Moffat Hills

Sundew

(otherwise known as *Drosera rotundifolia*)

What does it look like? Sundew is a tiny and delicate plant which is often overlooked. Its leaves are covered in sticky, red-tipped hairs. Small white flowers grow on a central stem, but seldom extend more than10cm high.

Where does it grow? Sundew loves the wet, so can be found almost anywhere that's damp, particularly on peaty soils that are low in nutrients, and around streams and flushes.

When can you see it? Most of the year, but it flowers between June and August.

What's so special about it? Sundew is a 'meat-eater'. It catches insects and uses their nutrients to compensate for the lack of nutrients found where it commonly grows. The glands at the tip of each leaf hair secrete a gluey liquid. This glistens like 'dew' attracting insects onto the sticky leaf where they become entombed and the nutrients absorbed. The 'dew' was once believed to take away warts and corns.

as botanists, nurserymen, specialist fern dealers and climbers arrived by train to collect it 🌟 *'Our*

be seen gracing a multicoloured carpet of bog mosses. The aptly named cloudberry is a characteristic plant of these North Pennine bogs. Bogs are common across the Lake District too, particularly on the undulating uplands between Thirlmere and Derwentwater and on the fells around Shap. Such places also provide excellent shelter for ground-nesting birds like the golden plover and dunlin. The streams and flushes which emerge from bogs often diversify their flora, providing a home for plants such as starry saxifrage and butterwort.

Ledge vegetation on Helvellyn

Oblong-leaved sundew

Life on the edge

To survive since the last age whilst under siege from the combined forces of changing climate, advancing woodland, smothering bog and munching animals, most of Cumbria's arctic-alpine flora has been forced to take drastic measures. Its survival strategy has been to retreat to locations like steep ledges, cliffs, gills and gullies, where competition for essential light, nutrients and space is less.

Englishmen nowadays set very much by it and holde it good for consumptions and swouning and faintness

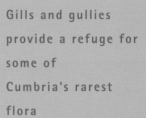

Gills and gullies provide a refuge for some of Cumbria's rarest flora

Lingmell Gill, Wasdale

of the harte, but I have no experience of this, neither have I red of anye writer what vertues it hath,

heather

lichen

mosses

berries

Below left: A mountain hawkweed

Below middle: Mountain sorrel

Below right: Roseroot

These plants can tolerate the harsh conditions found in such places and have literally hung onto life there, in some cases for over 10,000 years. Such locations have also discouraged grazing animals and plant collectors.

Again, not any old ledge will do, it has to be a ledge with the right sort of soil, further increasing the challenge of survival. The rarity of this flora of the fells attracted the Victorian plant-hunters who made the first full record of Cumbria's mountain plants. Unfortunately, they also enjoyed uprooting them to grow in gardens and nurseries and for their collections; an unhelpful activity in the plants' struggle for life.

The best examples of 'life on the edge' habitats are in the Lake District. On the eastern crags of Helvellyn,

wherefore I dare promise nothing of it', William Turner writing about sundew in his 'Herbal' published

The plant collector

John Balfour was a plant-hunter. Professor of Botany at the University of Edinburgh, Regius Keeper of the city's Royal Botanic Gardens and a founder member of its Botanical Society, he was a heavyweight Victorian collector. On July 21st 1853 Balfour came south to Ambleside, bringing a party of students with him for a lightning raid on the Lakeland fells. You had to be committed to tour with Balfour. The next day at 4.30 a.m. his party set out on a short ramble to Stockghyll Force for a spot of botanising before breakfast. Then it was a brisk walk through Rydal, Grasmere and up and over Dunmail Raise, before ascending Helvellyn from Wythburn.

A thick mist had enveloped the party by the time they reached the summit and cleared only as they had begun to descend Swirral Edge. Upon the cry of 'To the summit!' they retraced their steps. On arrival they were clearly in high spirits. Balfour records his difficulty in describing 'the ecstasy of the party as scene after scene opened up to their delighted eyes; when the whole mountainous district was discerned by them, their enthusiasm rose to the highest pitch'.

Riding on the crest of this wave of elation, his party set about the job in hand and began some serious plant-hunting on the cliffs below the summit between Swirral Edge and Striding Edge. The list of specimens his students gathered reads like a who's who of rare species and plants. The culprits are even named in some instances. Mr Cowan is said to have collected alpine saxifrage, which is now known only to occur in clusters of less than six plants at two places in Cumbria. Meanwhile, Mr Soubki was busy collecting alpine hawkweed, still rare to the county. Others had to settle for samples of purple saxifrage, various clubmosses and dwarf juniper. The following day they headed off to Ullswater, before returning north of the border with their trophies. Thankfully, recent legislation means that such activities are now illegal.

in 1568 ❀ *Cattle of a female kind are stirred up to lust by eating even a small quantitie', Thomas*

Mountain Avens

(otherwise known as *Dryas octopetala*)

What does it look like? Mountain avens has wiry stems with dark green leaves that carpet the ground. In season, white-petalled, anemone-like flowers break out on stalks up to 8 cm long.

Where does it grow? It is now extremely rare in Cumbria, growing only in a few places on the crags and cliffs of Helvellyn and Scafell.

When can you see it? If you can find it, it flowers in June and July.

What's so special about it? It is one of the true survivors of the flora of the fells and has probably been with us since before the last ice age. At one time it was so prolific that it even has a glacial period, the Dryas, named after it. More at home in the Arctic, it is a highly sensitive plant needing cool temperatures and high rainfall to keep it going.

Gerard, seventeenth century botanist on the aphrodisaic qualities of sundew 🌼 *"Tis good for spitting of*

Fairfield and High Street, among the shady cliffs can be found rare wonders like alpine saxifrage and mountain avens. Clusters of moss campion eke out a vertiginous existence beside tufts of purple saxifrage, roseroot, spring sandwort and mountain sorrel.

The damp ledges on Honister Crags are so rich in flora that they have been christened the hanging gardens of Lakeland. Here is a rich community of colourful plants like wood cranesbill, globeflower, goldenrod, marsh hawksbeard and wild angelica.

Ferns are also lovers of shady, rocky places. In the great chasm of Piers Gill on Scafell, beech and oak ferns grow alongside arctic-alpines. Parsley fern holds its own on the stony screes overlooking Wastwater and where screes are more blocky, scaly male-fern and the rare northern buckler fern may be seen.

Dwarf juniper clings on to a ledge

Blood, and Convulsions, and for Gripes. Outwardly applied, it cures Headaches, and Giddiness; and disposes

The Decision-Maker

My enthusiasm for things botanical began at primary school, and a botany degree seemed a logical progression. The first year at university was spent studying 'Lower Plants'. These are the often overlooked species of mosses, liverworts, ferns and fungi. A stay at Coniston Copper Mines Youth Hostel enabled me to see these wonderful plants in their natural habitat for the first time establishing an interest which has remained with me ever since.

High rainfall and a varied rock type makes the Lake District a magical place for the lover of lower plants. Screes, rock faces, gills, mires and the open fell provide prime habitats. Walls, such an important landscape feature, form an additional haven for mosses and liverworts.

The lower plants, like clubmosses, provide one of the most interesting, yet rarely noticed groups of flora of the fells. Six of Britain's seven species of clubmoss grow in the Lake District. They are ancient plants, not related to mosses or ferns, and have no flowers, reproducing instead by means of spores. Rarely 25 cm tall their larger relatives flourished, 250 million years ago, in the Carboniferous Period. They were so prolific then that their remains provided us with coal.

Found at over 900 m on Scafell Pike, clubmosses are true mountain plants and, although perhaps less attractive than more brightly coloured flowering plants, add an unusual dimension to our mountain flora. My job as a National Park Authority member is to ensure that changes to the National Park protect the landscapes where both these curious plants of the past and our more well-known flora grow.

Duncan Jeffrey,
Lake District National Park Authority member

adapted to the cold and windswept conditions. But the extensive, deep carpets of them, which once existed, have long been eroded through overgrazing by sheep.

Pause on your quest for the summit and you will see that any plants which grow here seem to do so in miniature. Pint-sized dwarf willow and juniper shelter amongst the boulders and hidden still further are the curious clubmosses, whose ancestors are almost as old as the hills themselves.

Woolly-hair moss on scree beside Crummock Water   **Walkers often miss what's under their feet**

Tough at the top

The Cumbrian mountains may not reach as high as the Alps, with only a handful of peaks rising more than 900m. However, they can be harsh places and the flora has had to adapt to the severe conditions. The barren moss and lichen-covered boulder fields are the most common landscapes on the highest tops. These are places for special types of plants which are well-

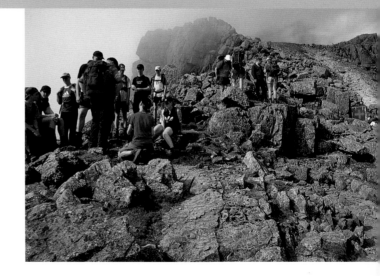

blows/Where oxlips and the nodding violet grows', William Shakespeare's 'A Midsummer Night's

Flush   Bog   Summit   Heath

The Future

The flora of the fells is one of Cumbria's richest assets. The remarkable story of its journey touches upon every aspect of the mountain landscape. The shape of the land, the nature of the geology, the type of climate and the impact of man have all played their part.

Since the end of the last ice age, when arctic-alpine flora thrived, the landscape has been changing. As opportunities arose, different flora established new communities, joining the arctic-alpine flora in the battle for survival in the Cumbrian uplands.

Each new community has had to compete for space and nutrients with those already established and it is this continual challenge which drives the wheels of change in our mountain landscapes.

Clearly today's landscape is only an echo of that of the past and the richness of the flora of the fells a shadow of what it once was. But the purple saxifrage thriving in the depths of Piers Gill on Scafell Pike illustrates the tenacity of Cumbria's mountain flora. The ice age may be history, but many of the arctic-alpine species which flourished in its wake are still with us, woven into our mountain landscapes alongside plants which have arrived more recently.

Things may not be perfect for the flora of the fells, sometimes pushed to the brink of extinction, but there is still hope for recovery. The landscape is always evolving and, with the increasing value we are now giving to wildlife, it is not too late to herald the return to a brighter, richer and more diverse day.

Dream' ❋ *Tormentil roots give a reddish-brown dye, hence a local name 'blood root'*

The Scafell range from Swirl Ho